AMERICAN SEX TAPE™

WISCONSIN POETRY SERIES

Sean Bishop and Jesse Lee Kercheval, series editors
Ronald Wallace, founding series editor

AMERICAN SEX TAPE™

JAMEKA WILLIAMS

The University of Wisconsin Press

Publication of this book has been made possible, in part, through support from the Brittingham Trust.

The University of Wisconsin Press
728 State Street, Suite 443
Madison, Wisconsin 53706
uwpress.wisc.edu

Gray's Inn House, 127 Clerkenwell Road
London EC1R 5DB, United Kingdom
eurospanbookstore.com

Printed in the United States of America
This book may be available in a digital edition.

Library of Congress Cataloging-in-Publication Data

Names: Williams, Jameka, author.
Title: American sex tape / Jameka Williams.
Other titles: Wisconsin poetry series.
Description: Madison, Wisconsin : The University of Wisconsin Press, [2022] | Series: Wisconsin poetry series
Identifiers: LCCN 2022013230 | ISBN 9780299340841 (paperback)
Subjects: LCGFT: Poetry.
Classification: LCC PS3623.I55677 A84 2022 | DDC 811/.6—dc23/eng/20220415
LC record available at https://lccn.loc.gov/2022013230

to my parents & Nancy Thomas

—*you will never die, you will live forever*

Let the priests tremble, we're going to show them our sexts!

—HÉLÈNE CIXOUS

CONTENTS

American Sex Cento   3

Scopophilia

"People are dying, Kim"   7

Intelligent Women   8

Brief Notes on the End of the World, Women   9

The All-American Girl   11

"But maybe boredom is erotic, when women do it, for men"   12

Plastic White Girl   13

I Intend to Outlast   15

Consider an Animal   16

Ignition   17

"There's a lot of baggage that comes with us, but it's like
    Louis Vuitton baggage (you always want it)"   19

Black, or Apologies for the Line "Sally Hemings in Leggings"   21

The All-American Girl   23

New Black Venus   24

My Sister Says ("Everyone can catch this smoke")   25

Original Sin   28

The Kardashians for a Better America   30

American Sex Tape   31

Black, or Even Now I Eat Like a Butcher's Dog   33

Birth of the Nation   36

Scopophobia

I'm Not the Queen of the Selfie   39

Woman Devours His Gaze   43

This World Is Not Good   44

Black, or I Sit on My Front Porch in the Projects, Waiting on God 46

Erotic Women Do It 47

"Now that I've survived, when does living begin?" 48

The Future Is Female 50

Black, or There Is No Nation Both Under God & Above Ground 51

Who Will Save Kim Kardashian? 52

I Intend to Outlast 53

War & Marriage 56

The All-American Girl 57

#Free Britney, Brittany, Britnée & Brittani, Too 58

Black, or The Natural World Doesn't Know Me 59

Nothing Is Promised 60

"I can't dwell?!?" 62

The New Me 64

The All-American Girl 65

"The new american girl doll is no longer a slave" 66

Since I Laid My Burden Down 67

Acknowledgments 69

Notes 73

AMERICAN SEX TAPE™

AMERICAN SEX CENTO

I hear America singing *you are the one*.
I am lit for the whole boatload of sensitive bullshit.
An artfully placed penis swung from the end
Of a rope like a flag.
Mossy and thumping,
Bare of logic,
Red.

I love you flesh into blossom, Empty Eagle.
Devouring all in haste.
Destroyer. Builder.
I'm totally into strapping on the belt of dynamite
In helpless, trembling bondage.

The Free? Who said the Free? Not me?
I never understood desire until I felt Your hands
Around my throat. You may stand upon me,
But do not hide Your face.
Can't find what You can't see, can You?

America, the beautiful night
Is about to blow up.
When the apocalypse comes
So will we.

SCOPOPHILIA

—I love to watch—

I'll cry at the end of the day, not with fresh makeup.
—KIM KARDASHIAN

"PEOPLE ARE DYING, KIM"

you get it
people are always getting themselves
ruined & my God especially the girls

keeled over on spring mattresses, pressed
from behind, guts distended with stars

but you despise waste: a diamond earring lost
to the ocean equals exactly one exquisite head
her mouth plastered shut

damn girl it's all good

you've worn the difference between death & dying
thrown death's cocaine-white pelt over your shoulders
cancer dissolved your father

are you not supposed to mourn
everything

starve your guts to pay debts or drink Detroit tap
someone has to enjoy God when he arrives

See Him a stripped vulva shined with SPF 30
See Him foaming & swirled in your lover's mouth
See Him sun-kissed thighs & brined fingertips
See Him stitched through the ears a sunken treasure.

INTELLIGENT WOMEN

Evoke the ghost of Plath.   Remember her body?
Charged with the glory of a god who is corruptible.
This corpse likes to touch her pink alone
& watch car crashes online.

Plath knew a pound of flesh equals pounds of flesh.
Dragging her ennui from room to room,
closets & corners   cow-heavy.

She & I are unwieldy, unwilling.

Show me one hundred of me
& I'll take my one hundred selves
to screw tight the lightbulb.

I draft suicide notes
for the intelligent women
I could never be.

   Salutations:
   I am: Artemis   A ball of clay   Mary Magdalene
   I sleep alone   An evening witch in rain
Gutted girl

                        Liturgy
                                Funeral
                                      America.

BRIEF NOTES ON THE END OF THE WORLD, WOMEN

I stepped on my mother's back
& Earth cracked open.
Flames chewed the hills.

During drought Black kids in Michigan
sank to the bottoms of public pools.
Their bellies bulged with lead.

⫿⫿⫿

God's unending ire never stops,
rolls over me in mysterious ways.

For example: some men have never
drowned in a real woman.
He climbed inside me hunting
for a fresh spring sighing

You don't feel
how I dreamed
you'd feel.

⫿⫿⫿

On the El train a lady instructs me
to spit into my hands. She thinks
my diseases will moisturize
my angry palm lines.

I'm still so heavy in the mornings
with plastic rings, aluminum cans.
But I never stop running over,
floating to the tops
of cocktails.

֍

In factories in the Valley, engineers
replicate vulvae in molds.
Eyeballs swim in vats of wax.

Mega-gallons of water filtered
in search of the perfect shade of nipple.
America! Make me impervious to death!

Wooden mouth.
Piano wire thong.
Three love holes.

Waterproof.

THE ALL-AMERICAN GIRL

First Date

How many women fit on your tongue?
Swear to God. Point a loaded gun
to your head. No bullshit. Tell me then
how come you're so alive, me—so dead?

"BUT MAYBE BOREDOM IS EROTIC, WHEN WOMEN DO IT, FOR MEN"

Kim worships our god: the god of snow

    & the god of fucking the god of bronzing moisturizers the god of grainy iPhone
footage the god who invented Black men the god of no bad publicity

    she is an indestructible object

    the god of softcore the god who wears waist-trimmers & two faces
the god of curled penises eclipsing marbled thighs the god of x-ray vision

    who made his children lustful who will be here recording her when she
cries when she thinks she is wasting into nothingness & that god
    will record   & do nothing

    the god of old magic tricks (here she is! here she is not!)
the god of thankless sacrifice the god who told her to smile who told her nipples *Smile!*
the god of what-goes-around-comes-back   the god of a body

    which cannot be ruined

who asks if we think she is harming The Culture who asks if we think
she is being used   who wonders what her children think

    god says Yes Yes even when the answer is

PLASTIC WHITE GIRL

White guys online want me savage,
draped in beads. Long black nipples
& nothing else.

ıı|ı

Do not hold me to the light.
I have a lot of browning thorns.

ıı|ı

Skinned & kinked.
Sally Hemings in leggings.

ıı|ı

In *Pinky*, Pinky Johnson passes for White.

ıı|ı

Nina Simone's skin was black & slick
with gin sweats. A furious drunk, she never
got a pair of blue eyes for Christmas.

ıı|ı

Don't leave me, my love.
Tangle your fingers here:
dark roots meet alabaster skull
(deletes Tinder account).

ıı|ı

I received a bar of Ivory soap &
a washcloth for Christmas one year.
A plastic white girl the next.

⍾

Gin is also white.
Simone's teeth: white.

⍾

I'm drunk. The white walls vibrate
like mice.

⍾

Simone sang of four women: *My name is Aunt Sarah!*
Sarah's skin: yellow. Her father: rich.
Her mother's skin:
forced.

⍾

My Sarahs are sweet milk rippling on the surface of a latte.
My Sarahs get DNA tests for their birthdays to see
if they have a little Wakanda in them
on their mama's side.

⍾

Spoiler alert: Pinky puts on the wrong skin.

I INTEND TO OUTLAST

I am not the same machine, which came rambling
off the conveyor belt, hugging the bolts & wires
spilling from her vivisection. I'm last year's model
with a sleeker softer system of cool disdain for
my Internet addictions. My mind sound as the wax
of a plaintive tree with supple leaves & syrup
for squirrels in autumn. Except my principles
are like post-op euphoria. My outrage
is hospital-humming. My eyesight's waves
break gold & purple like the L.A. Lakers.
I calmly ask my white nurse to tell my demons
to stop screaming. & *everything Black, I root for.*
& when they carved me open anything left inside
to corrode me (these dark braided sutures softened
like pouring tap into Lake Michigan) I tolerated.
Last year's model has the same speed as the year
with unending calamity. My fat featured tongue.
I'm trapped behind the glass of the discount case.
Everything tolerated.

I never learned the word escape.

CONSIDER AN ANIMAL

lives behind your eyes / eating pissing sleeping / in your head / Drags broken fingernails along your optic nerves / Screams all day / every night / She wants to fuck / but there is no one fucking / (short needles of black hair trail down her navel to a tuft of wool) / She wants to eat (something with sinewy flesh) / but no one is here to get eaten / You catch a shy guy on the El / he smiles in your direction / He has fragile eyes / The animal inside you says / you cannot have that / (You cannot have: sugarmoneyblood) / She wants a peanut butter sandwich / one Tuesday afternoon / You gargled fistfuls of peanuts between sobs / You sink shots of vodka / retching / The animal says she needs fresh air / & she wants to get out / & walk across your epidermis / You want to carve a road down the fine line / of the vein of your right wrist / Instead you etch six short trails in your forearm / because you don't want her to leave / She's been fun / Stay / A little blood / will suffice / She flies off kicking / into your brain stalk / wailing / all be damned

IGNITION

Open wide text me
your fevers chat me
up about our lonely
childhoods spent
flicking lit matches
at chained dogs kick
up the flames with
wrap your mouth
around or melt to
your knees sing for
me I am alone I am   lonely!
as the moon is faithful
always singing self-pity
to American Dream eyes
& megapixel bathroom
bod or guy in bowtie
dreaming of digital
porn still-life his desires
as pretty as a potted plant
in front of an oiled pair
of tits amalgamations
of the men my father
wants me to cook dinner
for when the microwave
is all that's left
to buzz between us   *Sing!*

flicker like flames of broken
code raining down screen
my mainframe teeth & addled
analog mouth yearning is not
a private affair your mother
has alone in the bathroom
running her fingers down
her throat   so how will
our children know we
were here, bloody & wet,
simulacrum lovers? chain
ourselves outside & howl
wagging our extinguisher
tongues?

"THERE'S A LOT OF BAGGAGE THAT COMES WITH US, BUT IT'S LIKE LOUIS VUITTON BAGGAGE (YOU ALWAYS WANT IT)"

I pray for my maids their gods
have more debt than my god
my god has more favor more
sex appeal do not misunderstand
I take time for myself burning
my silk sheets one thread at a time
I call the president & I ask if money
corrupts absolutely I chew TV
noise & eat expensive corpses
there's a particular way in which
men are hypnotized click me
press your hard thumb to my lips
or décolletage & you think you've
burned a cross into my forehead
you think my various holograms
are possessed fucking the camera's
brains loose but honestly my spare
time is spent focusing my energies
on not disappearing. I count the pixels
of my breasts I tolerate my reflection
I sweat the calories from my heart
I buy my corset & coffin wholesale
I give shit away I let my husband
serenade my vagina I sing lullabies
to my children long after they've

faded I edit the martyrdom I remove
the cameras from my home I invite
cameras back inside I leak to the lenses

I thrive.

BLACK, OR APOLOGIES FOR THE LINE "SALLY HEMINGS IN LEGGINGS"

I think a lot about empires.
& how am I supposed
to finish erecting this one?

In the footnotes there is always just-some
Black woman squatting in sodden clay,
her blustering body birthing planters,
partitioners & prophets.

Give her flowers while she's alive
to smell them. Just once.
Then let them wilt a slow rot.

Stinks sweet like the guiltiest of parties
rolling up their sleeves
to reveal fake plastic roses
hidden in the crooks of their elbows.

There were two Monticellos.
Only one came true.
Where a war of chokecherry trees
flowered in her blood.

Wherever you trek dominions grow.
& if your kin bleed out
this nation's throat is slashed.

& children of ghosts squabble
over who laid the first brick.
But who cut off the hand
of the man who laid
the first brick?

THE ALL-AMERICAN GIRL

Sext message no. 3

Let me push here where your world
begins. Your tongue kicking
my knuckle. Don't dare. I'll hold
your breath on my fingernail.

NEW BLACK VENUS

When a Black woman starves
she eats the fat of my ass dips
her cornbread in the oil pressed
from my pores my table stays set
for famine well-nourished in body
my nipples point north to a vigilant
god from which the manna rains
she asks why some women are born
last & so far from God I say my trues-
come-dream L.A. wasn't built in a day
but on a waxed million-dollar vagina
mouths claim they never had a _____ girl
like me & I let my glitter splatter their beards
white girls say when I go blonde I'm like
a whole other ethnicity so exotic like
some pets & dancers I forget that Black
women have happened to me & men
& sex have happened to them but
sister says more more of *that*: my skin
the New Black my Venus is a Persian rug
on collection dreams gestate & die
between my lips center of the universe
toll the bell who wants to dine first

MY SISTER SAYS
("EVERYONE CAN CATCH THIS SMOKE")

A gun is a magic wand.

A bullet disappears inside a man's chest
faster than a hand clears smoke
from the end of a cigarette.

So when my sister says she will hunt the man who pushed me into the concrete █████████
████████████ she has a trick up her sleeve.

Penn & Teller perform a magic trick,
more accurately, an illusion. Mute Teller shoots
verbose Penn in the mouth with a handgun.

Penn smiles. Clenched between his teeth: a gold bullet.
Its butt caved by the hammer but otherwise clean, glinting.
Penn, for the record, does not believe in miracles.

But like Christ, Penn & Teller perform anti-death.
Some kind of gods.

("The depressed person is a radical, sullen atheist.")

████████ my sister says █████ hunt the man ███████████████████
████████████████████████████████

⫘

Merriam-Webster:
i.   To pursue—

25

ii.   To pursue *with intent to capture*
iii.   To traverse *in search of prey*

(inside you will find me eating entire black suns.

████████████████████ man ██████ me in ████ concrete ██████
██████████ she ████████████████████████

████████████████████ man ██████████ me in ████ concrete ██████
██████████ me ████████████████████████

        a black sun.   inside.
you will find.   a black sun.   split me.)

(Kristeva: "Naming suffering, exalting it, dissecting it into its smallest components—that is
     doubtless a way to curb mourning.")

When my sister says she will
traverse
intent to
capture
prey

            (who split me)
I have to make believe she will.

                                        She eats the sun performs his death.

A gun is magic   (I do not believe in spells & incantations).

A sullen atheist, I enjoy
the language of violence.
The way it bounces
across my tongue
between my teeth.

The rhetoric of vengeance
(& the Lord shall have *It*)
in the female mouth
can be unctuous.

Revenge fantasy.
Teeth clenched down
on an Adam's apple.
Clean, glinting.

But, of course, there is no God.

Penn's blown-out teeth.

I blink the illusion of death away.

⫴

My sister & I are in
Walmart shopping
for pistols. Our black
pupils bright with
swelling conviction.

She grips a gun
as easy as holding
a flat iron to her scalp.

"Tell me what
he looks like,"
she'll say.

I say: (Everyone.)

ORIGINAL SIN

Philosophers say Eve's original sin
is her ambition. Scholars respond:
her original sin is her curiosity.
Political historians recommend
that the global crisis of sin did not
begin with an American red apple
as we are made to believe, lustrous & smutty,
like the fruit the witch paints with poison
in the Disney classic *Snow White*.
But it was Arabic figs, honey-like
& floral, that doomed Woman.
But the atheists say her original sin
is that she believed in God.

In her exotic drunkenness, Eve
discovers her blue eyes & ivory skin are actually
dark brown. She looks down at her navel & thinks
it should be gemmed & exposed in music videos.
Eve can feel her nipples! For the first time!
Theologians suggest Eve wants vision & that is folly.
Cultural critics scoff & denounce: Eve has a sweet tooth.

& as if she has the Redeemer's eyes herself
she can see the future scheme unfurl before her.
A conspiracy of babies lunging ravenously
for her weeping swollen tits, men plotting
to record her dancing in a wet t-shirt with an app.

Everyone scratches until blood to possess
what she so courageously wrenched from
the tree of the knowledge of good and evil.
Consider the poverty of testosterone.
A fate of secondary citizenry.
The Creator's soft parenthesis for an illiterate Adam.
Eve wants to be seen & that is human nature.
Agnostics know her original sin is that God
comes & goes as He pleases.
God turns His face from her to Adam.
She vomits her applesauce.

THE KARDASHIANS FOR A BETTER AMERICA

Kim Kardashian: Hollywood™

eat soup over the corpses of Black lovers   suffer their cocaine addictions   all awash in
lube   lidocaine aglow in the gums   teeth brighter than tequila   wearing a white
membrane on that tight brown body   Coco Chanel cape/for sex tomorrow night   corset-
thin/like a victim   crawling through spoon shots of silicon dioxide   cut with honey
read the green tea leaves:

                              i'm not depressed anymore i just have desires
            my psychiatrist
                                        says
            to exfoliate
                        better

My avatar smiles back
she & i cry like real
humans do

AMERICAN SEX TAPE

THE SEQUEL: /

    Haunt a talk show this morning/
    Kiss a soldier on his cheek center stage

/You are the love of his life/

    He folds you up, doll/
    slides you into the pocket of his shorts/

    You must rise to every occasion/
    Sneeze a few million dollars before dinner/
    Keep fans/
    from coming all over you/   paradise the boredom   TAKE #0032:/

    Acknowledge a cage of mirrors/
    Sleep off the demons in the backseat of a tinted Lexus/

(entertainment-interrogation-interlude:

how often do you scratch yourself

from the official record of your life?/

your tongue is ghost-like or godly?)

With gold stars you purchase a puppy/
He sleeps alongside you/
In frightened snatches:

        Kimoji™ blinks
        Me seminatrix   tentacles   dancing

BLACK, OR EVEN NOW I EAT LIKE A BUTCHER'S DOG

Even now with *this* black body is not
& *that* black body is not too
Even though black bodies
are born
obstetricians noose the umbilical cords
& black babies grow to be big & black
& decay   at the same exact time
& black like eggplant black
like your father's diabetic brother   black
& frying eggplant splattering oil
hit the knuckles
burn like nothing   my mother says
& black don't hurt
but black & hungry
& black & thirsty for Kool-Aid
& black & drunk as hell
Even now with black split between
sleeping

                                        & fading away
with all the black & walking going on around here
with all the black & jogging
& black feet ashy & too fast   strike a match
big girl's good slippers

        up
        in flames
& black   & running   away
&   sulfur   in the kicked-up dust

Even now with all the black
& selling loosies
& black & counterfeit
& black & moving
the hands up
& moving the hands
to the sides
& black & let me
see your hands   & black
& eating
& black &
I got change right here sir
& black &
let me see
your hands
Even though there's black
& getting married & still black
& black & has a mortgage
                    & still black
& black & invested in the future   (what

                              future?)
& still black   as   fuck
& black & raised
    private school pickaninnies

              & still still still

                        & still

Even now I, unremarkable darkie
              mammy pleasant
                    voodoo queen,
I slide back
onto my haunches

a great sphinx
turning my Egyptian nose
to the moon
& I eat
like a butcher's dog

BIRTH OF THE NATION

. . . & then the erotic self begun. The pink parts shut-up in the eternal & the jealous. Obsidian unfurls its wet petals. Composure divine as a crown of snakes synchronized uncoiling witnesses the male animal become marble. In bed. Amaranthine. Midnight's moaning music sweeps. Slaves become diplomats. Apple pie drools its spiced sap. Blue jeans are caked in the muds made of lynched sons' piss. Keep it. If fucking is like the founding of an empire, let us love like we are the patient American bison, lumbering towards hysterical extinction, from the eastern seaboard to the Rockies, ecstatic & grieving at once that we have run out of country over which to drag our vulgar bellies.

SCOPOPHOBIA

—*I cannot look*—

Give them pleasure. The same pleasure they have when they wake up from a nightmare.
—ALFRED HITCHCOCK

I'M NOT THE QUEEN OF THE SELFIE

(nowhere can you find
my likeness on anything
of value

I have a job

I take medication
for nightmares
difficult to pronounce

I'm not in stilettos
and Balmain latex
all month y'know

won't catch me dining
with legislators on behalf
of Black girls in lockdown
for slicing daddy or pimp

selling the footage
of my re-education
to the highest bidder

ask me about genocides
Armenian or American
or otherwise

& I'll admit
my eyes
were closed

won't cry
for the first
or future husbands

stopped crying
about the first rape

forgave myself
for self-harm

& I'm beating
the sin out of
a reality TV star

there's no room left
in my heart to store
the acid, the venom

& I won't abandon
my Black friends
with XOXO

—I'm unphased
like the moon
& western politics

as long as white women's
nipples peek through
bohemian blouses
the Queen of the Selfie
will continue to shine
on the Empire of Man

& I mean all of us
even my niggas

but I do have nice things
like the Queen

Kim & I share
the same unforgivable ass
& a talent for fits
of mourning

& the 2.0s of ourselves
I call them minor prophets
or minor prostitutes

in reality like me
Kim never leaves
her settee

afraid to witness
how God has failed
poor brown women
again

so we're eyes-wide-shut
masturbating to pixels
of Jolies & Chads

when we can manage
the trembling in our hands

tears lubricating the leather
fetal, folding in front of laced tea

in our chambers
alone

I believe that God created
Kim on the first day & everything
He built upon her:

with a yawn she stretches a T
like a.crucifix as the servants
draw the curtains & she slithers
into her latex & kitten heels
to keep this empire
from drowning)

& I can't remember joy either.

WOMAN DEVOURS HIS GAZE

Stripped to bare feet
oil caps her hips
lips rich in protein
& Hennessy (he won't
drink anything lighter
than him / she swallows
nothing darker)
sigmoid spine
redacted black pubes
why should you be
a veiled woman?
because men are
cameras?
& what do we expect
to dream of you?
stigmata where
there should be navel
or nipples heavy
with mother's milk?
understand this: a woman
is a narrow well
& man groans to fill her
then man voids
himself / woman
devours his gaze

THIS WORLD IS NOT GOOD

Especially to Kim Kardashian tender
as an egg, crying, her mouth a busted yolk

would eat her roasted placenta three meals a day
to heal the heart-shaped ache in her belly

she asks if there's too much beauty in her diet
imagines her kidneys growing eyelashes, polished fingernails

why are the appetizers the shape of bullets
her meals fluttered or moaned once, having known fear.

She sees the seabass wink before her chef lops him in two
she wonders aloud should Apocalypse come will we try to eat her

what color does starvation come in anyhow
how many loaves of bread can we break from her body

will famine reduce men to their essentials: salt & semen
what makes some women all steeled bone or chagrin

won't she become gossamer, our last mother to suckle & teethe
how many licks does it take to get to the center of her soul.

This world, regrettably, is poor with explanations.
If the End should come tomorrow, Kim concludes,

I will give them just a little taste of my pain
served only on Hermès dinner plates.

BLACK, OR I SIT ON MY FRONT PORCH IN THE PROJECTS, WAITING ON GOD

& when she arrived she did not disappoint. Her low-hanging breasts; the nipples puffy & down-turned. The smile of gapped teeth fed with coconut oil & a side of fried okra. She petted my wooly head, ran her swollen knuckles down my bitter spine & recoiled. Cursed the weight of my sorrow with hymns. Why is there no milk or honey in you, child? God asked & I said I burn I cry what's new. God scoffed. How many wars did Helen fuel with her labia? Her will? She answered: exactly the number she needed to win men to their deaths. I interrogated. Does God have a pussy where her soul should be? I keep it in a vanity box, she said, with my menopause & my pocket change & my wit. Then suddenly I remembered being a girl of ten climbing the stairs of my grandmother's house on Potter Street. In her bedroom, I cracked the spine of her jewelry box studded with broken sequins like baby's teeth. I clasped her pearl earrings, her needles, threads, her shards of glass in between my hands for supplication declaring that I hold a woman like a man should. Then God placed my hands on her face & I thumbed the wrinkles across her eyebrows & down her cheeks & she said that that was Woman. & then I rubbed the pouch in which her children drowned & she said that that was Woman also. & she unveiled a torn hymen, a full beard, the collapse of the old gods of sex & declared that this can be Woman too. & she placed a hand inside the lacunae where my heart should be & said I was Woman too. & who says God is cruel & without color?

EROTIC WOMEN DO IT

An erasure

she is an Indestructible Object
two faces eclipsing

       his recording

she is   she is   *that* god.

the old tricks sacrifice her

      the god of ruined Culture.

she wonders what

god says

"NOW THAT I'VE SURVIVED, WHEN DOES LIVING BEGIN?"

To my knowledge, I have not slept with someone's husband.

Ass like a tailored lawn in Kenilworth. A straight-A student.

Intellect like *Another trillion-plus to the debt ceiling?*

Due to my mythic endurance, one can liken me to an onyx marble slab central

to a tax-funded memorial garden, waxed over with smears & gnawed gum.

My eyes stoned into eternal reverence for this haunted earth.

It is never enough to cup my screams in my hands.

The neighbor's toddler always startles, bolts into peals of his own hunger.

It is never enough.

I deserve to inherit more than wind, more than Budweiser farts rolling over the amber waves.

What I'm saying is it is time to buy a gun.

& yoga in order to restore balance to my life.

I'm rubbing every amethyst in this white lady's crystal store.

All her good chakras & good sense depleted in a sneer.

With certainty, I am unable to claim that I exist, or if I am a shade in the corner

of someone's racial imagination.

Every master closes his eyes to dream of me & blankets of snowy static fall forever.

I thought I should have died—miserable miracle.

Benediction: enough good earth left to pull up over my shoulders.

Steal leftover clay & mold a future with which I can indict the American empire

on my mother's name.

There's a one-bedroom cottage downtown for me.

A toy dog leaping from my basket of sumo oranges.

Pissing on a suede Ugg boot by the door.

& I'm smiling at a cum stain on thousand-thread-count bedsheets.

Student debt is vacuuming my rugs.

Over the blare of Stevie Wonder's horns, white men buried under my house

yelp, bending the kitchen tiles with their erections.
I am a good girl
        —the spiked pin   on a blue ribbon.

THE FUTURE IS FEMALE

I know what the future holds.
America will throw me out
with the bathwater & bourgeoisie.
Deny my bowels, my clit.
Raise me by my hair roots & shear.
Set fire to my lawns
& my favorite salad joints.

In exchange for mercy I will offer
my tits, fat & happy, to Heaven.
Ask me to carry another woman's mattress
like a crucifix.
Can I kiss your children on their noses?
Let my lacquered lips be a consecration.

New viruses mature every year.
Dining & fucking with disregard,
chivalrously, will no longer suffice.
But how am I going to make money?
Will you sell me?
In what colors?

In this fantasia I sacrifice myself
with a face wiped clean.

I said I am not a feminist.
I mean I'm not running for president.

BLACK, OR THERE IS NO NATION BOTH UNDER GOD & ABOVE GROUND

I come from gravy stock. My father's laughter glutinous,
encouraged porridge. Shed his mask & there! A parrot's green
wings spread. & my mother—because the water is calm
doesn't mean crocodiles sleep. She is a full moon. The full moon
loves me. When they die campuses of libraries will burn.
The foundations will crackle & scream madsong in the cinders.
Roots shake off the ash, gasp for air. Old folks talk of trees.
Axes forget but the trees remember. Niggas talk of home.
There is no nation both under God & above ground. I come from
the afterbirth & the grave & all one must survive between them.
I am the blood sugar. I am the pistil.
I am the wild thing with the hot pink tongue.
& once you carry your own water
you will remember every drop.

WHO WILL SAVE KIM KARDASHIAN?

America is sicker than ever / white women need saving / & often /
a white woman drags / a Black rapper up the spire / of the Empire State Building /
Kim thinks this movie is boring / prefers tears in a champagne flute / makes love & war
in a few kilobytes / We admonish / Kim, what nice tits / you have /
drop / a guillotine / on your Gucci collar / hike up our petticoats /
& take your place / at the block /

(Look, Kim. All we ask is for our daughters to grow long daisy limbs
wearing miniskirts dyed short wavelengths. Their brown scalp grows
kinks blonder than bleach. A magic filter turns their dark eyes blue.
The sun & the moon follow our daughters home when white men kiss
them.)

White America has shown you / mercy /
go & do likewise /
& her tears are brackish /
but refreshing to you

I INTEND TO OUTLAST

I.

I wish there was an afterlife

              someplace to lift my chin towards

     I'm eating shit & running rabbits again

   & no longer interested in innocence

     never learned a thing

so jaded
my only hope
is in God
          or the city

                  & you look good to me,

             Chicago

     I leave my waking terrors on your blitzed shoulders.

Solitude is found
only where rats rest
their little engines
determined
to see another day
of starvation.

II.

The rats, they *see* me

    &

Lake Michigan & I are one-and-the-same

                big-bodied

                open

                cool for love

I've been thinned   dollar down

    stomach tightening
    around a

                single   can   of   tuna.

III.

a god amongst rabbits

chewing the fat

    I sing full-throated to Lake Michigan in the evenings

a little stoned & weepy

                but God rises

WAR & MARRIAGE

Is holding your hand extinction?
& won't that make me a bitter mouth
refusing to pair off until I have my milk?
Shoot in the belly anyone protecting their heart
that durable god who ticks down to the day
we are felled by war or marriage. Stand. Anyone?
& show me how one holds another's hand
without thinking: catastrophe.
The airplanes are hanging a little low.

If I spit blood into your palm & shake your hand
call it intimacy. Gestures of desire are sick
with the disease of life. Only freshly freed convicts
& poets understand. My silence is masturbation.
I open my mouth for celibacy's sake.
Am I really the only thing I own in this country?
Then what is left to tell? Nuclear shells & cockroaches
will bed down in the abandoned casts of our mattresses.
We will stand in the dark, our mirrors empty,
gladly performing for no one, bearing witness to nothing.

THE ALL-AMERICAN GIRL

Freudian slip

On the El I daydream I carve a man
from his membership screaming blood-drunk
Jesus Christ took the eunuch in his arms
& lined the man's pockets with condoms.

#FREE BRITNEY, BRITTANY, BRITNÉE & BRITTANI, TOO

One after another they descend Jacob's ladder rising from the smoke machine smog holding banana-gold pythons draped over their shoulders. They hold these slaves like an atlas. Men are held down with smooth lips gathering tenderness. Made slaves to a womanness against a championship of cock. Culling heat, vibrato. There is a jungle these women are in search of. They hold a lot of seeds which they forget to drop into the quaking earth. They are sorry. Not sorry. One says to the other sorry not sorry. One says this to another's shorn head. To a tramp stamp. To another one's flab. Apologizing to her bodies she attacks her captors with the hook of an umbrella. She wants to have sex right now. Wants to keep all the money she's made. She wants to be contemporary too & tear her Spanx at the belly & cool her titties in the shade the shade the shade. Holding hunger over their pythons these women bite down through ethernet chords. The snakes rebel. Floored a Black girl.

BLACK, OR THE NATURAL WORLD DOESN'T KNOW ME

& the natural world doesn't know he's white—sanctuaries
of oaks, brambles soaked in dog piss, goose shit in the grass
—they don't know.
The dumb dark heads of sunflowers bow to us. Bees siphon
the last liquors from stamens minding their damn business.
They all don't know me. Common yellowthroats, vibrant with
sex, flutter branch to branch, while my lips & his
—their hearts so small they don't beat but vibrate supernovic
like a foe of atoms on the head of a pin
—they don't know us.
Turned on by veins of wind.
Tuned into the hunger of strays. He & I are all of this.
This matters.
My ancestors' dangerous feet praised the soil.
Their mouths melancholia. The rattling black of captive crows.
Wit & wilderness in their skulls. Their backs the bark of red cedar,
bald cypress. Flowering dogwood they are. They don't know he's white.
Don't know his grandfather passed successfully. Fled north.
Light in his guts. Saw the rivers amniotic. Water is the womb of all
of these things. We in & of & are
in the deepest ocean   the bottom of the sea
in the deepest ocean   eaten by the worms
I'd be crazy not to follow   where you lead
& fall off.

NOTHING IS PROMISED

I'm a rare-r nigga now.   Eating sushi north side.
Turning my white loverboy out. I know only one mantra,
one psalm: nothing is promised. Your bitch is acting brand new
watching this roach ascend the French press, eating his crumb.

Like I wasn't him. But facedown on the hardwood.
My spirit small. Smaller than the passive crumb.
Nothing is promised.

& the white boyfriend? I hope he finds better. Green & blush & warm.
Someone messianic when she spreads her legs. When she opens her purse.

Forced to my knees, a rapist pawed my skull.
Suck me. Suck me, he whined. & there I was   nothing.
Now I put money in the ground because men have so much of it.
I put money in the ground because I have not enough.

Fuck money. I put it to bed. I put it to death.

Watch this bad bitch.
A Black bitch. Toothy. Wiping red from her slick,
Moorish mouth with hundred dollar bills. I love to see it.
I love to live inside that camera's orgasm.

The joy in her nihilism thrills the ape in me.
Why do I desire to view her sinking newly won fangs
into something still convulsing with the pure breath of promise?

We paid with our carcasses.
Cocky. Unruly. *Ain't none of us perfect.*
I hope it was worth it.

Let white ladies draw their children
& wallets into their stomachs
as we stalk the edges of your screen.

Yes! We could make change for you.
No. We're not sorry that all our bills are glossy
with your blood, viscid, freshly spilled.

"I CAN'T DWELL?!?"

Paris, at gunpoint

I'd like to sit
   on men's hunger in peace
      return their dull glares
         with cheekbones carved high
            wrap my loving embrace
               around their rib cages
                  buzzing with healthy eggs

my dumb hole
   my dumb lack
      dreams teenage boys suffer
        the same wet grave

I ask my gravedigger
   to carve me wide enough
      to swallow my enemies whole
        the dirt begs for her life
      ankles bound in the bathtub
of a nineteenth-century luxury hotel

a chain of men anoint my feet
   on my Instagram feed:
      we miss u
        we miss youuuu
      cum back to me :(:(:(

                        I send photocopies of myself
                        through electronic mail

I send myself.

kim pours you a glass of milk she kisses it
eyes open another kim licks all of your ice cream
kim stands in the shower while another stands
in your mirror tits bare one kim lays in your bed
freshly bronzed holding another kim under rains
of glitter & the glitter never falls or settles
the kims do not move their arms nor do any
other kims move their legs the kims do not
open their mouths we do not hear a thing
I sign

WISH I WAS HERE XO

THE NEW ME

He is a new creation; the old has passed away
2 CORINTHIANS 5:17

The new me means "to be new monied." Everything I've ever claimed, for it, I died. Which is to say my flesh is labor. The muscles of my back fan like wings. The rings of my neck open for low-wage toil anew. A valve in my heart opens its palms, burns up. Grows a replacement whenever my man spills his seed on my ribcage at the end of the workday. Everything that ever touched me is mine. Newborn brain cells curse the sum of my electric bills. Blood cells freeze in my swollen feet. I inherited the silhouettes of Jezebel or Mamie, but I'm still big booty trendy. A new me has replaced a haggard model that was too concerned with having polite skin. This prototype of me does not understand the old body's rape. Winces as if I've described a small critter struggling against the grip of some winged breed's talons on the National Geographic channel. This prototype can't be duped. The new me does not refurbish memories, but her onboard glitches now & again. Her tar-slick shell quivers at the re-memory of slave ships tossing on the choppy Atlantic. Textbook etchings of my extinct selves, chained throat-to throat, by force, at the mouths of muskets & men. All these me(s) waterlogged, eyes aflame with disbelief at the bottom of the Middle Passage. I'm sorry, America, but I'm rich in baby oil & paperback novels only these days. So finish paying for me with what is mint. No conditions.

THE ALL-AMERICAN GIRL

Sex tape, take no. 141

This high-rise is porn for jumpers
Herpes is forever
When we have sex, you flex, our spirit animals meet-cute in chatrooms
I think I gave you my social security number by accident

"THE NEW AMERICAN GIRL DOLL IS NO LONGER A SLAVE"

the gates are flung /
I dog the bones / worming gardens for sour fruits /
to drink / sticky stimulants / in the new throes /
busting rocks / with my teeth / my throat /
growing longer / a crane / I bleat /
my flower / has changed / her / veins /
arteries / of a map / the only out is through /
the trap / the mouth / the navel /
Sons of the Union! / having made me / post-existence /
any   thing / can / become / me /
I am hives / blooming red / across your chests /
a memory / a shock of spring sympathies / iced over /
half-monster / from the train tracks / slicking her fleas /
slut / skank / sphinx /
medusa / madonna / mammy /
with the right conditioning / you believe / I can /
show you / who you are & / a more perfect / union /
had you just known /
remained cautious /
you would have smelled me / coming /
I cradle your acute skull / slip my knife /
between rib & breathe / the horror / of my /
perfection /
I god you / I devil / dance / two caked feet /
little myths / prophecies from a tapping tongue /
now I get it / I understand / what liberty had always /
known /
I'm post-post colonial /

Sentenced to casually die, for I am forgiven.

SINCE I LAID MY BURDEN DOWN

I eat like I got Beyoncé shit to conquer
I grow my eyebrows furiously
I look at fucking & my genitals are not too cold
or too hot I feel as if I belong to myself
& I deserve sweatpants
I dream longer now since I've set it down
dreamed Christ blew a bunch of Black girls
goodbye kisses clenched his farewells
in my little fists I practiced repression
folding to my knees in the afternoons
serving an invisible crotch
one day called to serve at a man's zipper
& he won't know my name or eyes
my god unwind your ideologies
from around your ovaries
you will not be buried twice
be both thirsty & the flood
my swollen cloud cells pissed rain for days
whoever drowned was collateral
I don't set names to anyone or anything anymore
I just roll back into the sea
instead of my usual rage uncaught & dreaming:
just want to be Taylor Swift tomorrow
there will be money won't there be?

ACKNOWLEDGMENTS

Sincerest thanks to the editors of the following journals in which versions of these poems first appeared:

Black Warrior Review: "Nothing Is Promised"
Contemporary Verse 2: "American Sex Cento," "I Intend to Outlast ['I am not the same machine']."
Digging Press: "The New Me"
Gigantic Sequins: "This World Is Not Good"; "War & Marriage"
Gulf Coast: "Birth of the Nation"; "#Free Britney, Brittany, Britnée & Britanni, Too"
Jet Fuel Review: "Plastic White Girl"; "Consider an Animal"
Muzzle Magazine: "There's a lot of baggage that comes with us, but it's like Louis Vuitton baggage (you always want it)"
Oyez Review: "My Sister Says ('Everyone can catch this smoke')"
Painted Bride Quarterly: "The Kardashians for a Better America"
Powder Keg Magazine: "People are dying, Kim"; "New Black Venus"; "Woman Devours His Gaze"
Shrew Magazine: "Intelligent Women"; "The All-American Girl" sequence
Tupelo Quarterly: "Brief Notes on the End of the World, Women"; "Ignition"; "Since I Laid My Burden Down"
Yemassee Journal: "I can't dwell?!?"

"Black, or I Sit on My Front Porch in the Projects, Waiting, on God" was first printed in *Misrepresented People: Poetic Responses to Trump's America*, edited by María Isabel Álvarez and Dante Di Stefano (NYQ Books, 2018)

I extend my deepest and most heartfelt gratitude to the following people who have touched my life and the life of this manuscript over the course of several years.

The Master of Fine Arts in Prose & Poetry program at Northwestern University and the professors, classmates, and mentors there who gave me and this book rigorous instruction, dedicated time, and openness: Simone Muench, Rebecca Morgan Frank, Faisal Mohyuddin, and Ed Roberson. Thank you.

Sincerest gratitude to my undergraduate mentor who instilled within me a joy for craft: Nancy Thomas.

And to Joyce Munro, who upon her retirement gifted me a spectacular collection of poets reading verse across numerous vinyls and cassettes.

In the loving memory of Mr. Robert Walton, my high school English teacher, who taught me not only how to comprehend literature but how to hear every movement in the lines.

Brian Teare, Ronald Wallace, and Sean Bishop, thank you for championing this manuscript. I am forever grateful for the support of the Brittingham Trust and the astounding work of the University of Wisconsin Press.

I extend my full heart for the love of my first readers: Jimmia—my sister, my mirror, and my ride-or-die. My best friend and partner-in-pop-culture, Deanna Foley, whose unwavering enthusiasm for this book (and Kim Kardashian) kept me laughing and smiling through revisions. And my close friend, Dan Garner, whose insight and vision gave me confidence to write with greater artistic abandon.

To Eric, my weird fish, I fell for you while I wrote the last half of this book on your grandmother's couch. *Your eyes, they turn me . . .*

With respect and humility, I am thankful for the inspiration of several writers and muses. Their works have challenged me and shown me how art and language can transform:

The writers whose spoken or written words jump-started several of these poems: novelist Margaret Atwood; poets Derrick Austin, Tiana Clark, Ricky Laurentiis, Precious Okoyomon, and Morgan Parker; and writer/producer Issa Rae.

Hélène Cixous, Julia Kristeva, and Toni Morrison. Their philosophies of womanhood, art, and grief gave me ground on which to stand and imagine.

Solange Knowles, Noname, and Rihanna provided the soundtrack to my writing process.

And, of course, thank you, Kim Kardashian.

To my parents,
The first book is for you.
Your love
& sacrifices
have set me free.

NOTES

The sources for "American Sex Cento" are as follows:

"I Hear America Singing," Walt Whitman from *Leaves of Grass* (1860)

"To a dark moses," Lucille Clifton from *An Ordinary Woman* (Random House, 1974)

"Howl," Allen Ginsberg from *Selected Poems 1947–1995* (HarperPerennial, 2001)

"Penis Blues," Kim Addonizio from *My Black Angel: Blues Poems and Portraits* (Stephen F. Austin University Press, 2014)

"Some Advice to Those Who Will Serve Time in Prison," Nazim Hikmet from *Poems of Nazim Hikmet*, translated by Randy Blasing and Mutlu Konuk (Persea Books, 1994)

"Your Other Heart," Natalie Shapero originally published in the July/August 2012 issue of *POETRY*

"Recreation," Audre Lorde from *The Collected Poems of Audre Lorde* (W.W. Norton, 1997)

"Venus and Adonis," William Shakespeare from the first Quarto (1593)

"The Congressional Library," Amy Lowell from *What's O'Clock* (Houghton Mifflin, 1955)

"Climbing Everest," Frederick Seidel from *Ooga-Booga: Poems* (FSG, 2007)

"Servitude," Anne Reeve Aldrich from *The Rose of Flame and Other Poems of Love* (1889)

"Let America Be America," Langston Hughes from *The Collected Poems of Langston Hughes* (Alfred A. Knopf, 1994)

"Dirty Pretty Things," Michael Faudet from *Dirty Pretty Things* (Andrew McMeel Publishing, 2016)

"On the Pulse of Morning," Maya Angelou from *On the Pulse of Morning* (Random House, 1993)

"American History," Michael S. Harper from *Songlines in Michaeltree: New and Collected Poems* (University of Illinois Press, 2000)

"Patriotics," David Baker from *Like Thunder: Poets Respond to Violence in America*, edited by Virgil Suárez and Ryan G. Van Cleave, (University of Iowa Press, 2002)

"The Bones Below," Sierra DeMulder from *The Bones Below* (Write Bloody Publishing, 2010)

The opening epigraph is by French feminist philosopher Hélène Cixous, from the essay "The Laugh of the Medusa," translated into English by Keith Cohen and Paula Cohen, originally published by the University of Chicago Press (1976).

The epigraph of section one was spoken by Kim Kardashian on the reality TV show *Keeping Up with the Kardashians* ("Loving and Letting Go," season 9, episode 1).

The epigraph of section two by English filmmaker Alfred Hitchcock was stated to a reporter for the *Asbury Park Press*, printed on August 13, 1974.

"People are dying, Kim" is inspired by a now infamous incident in *Keeping Up with the Kardashians* ("Trouble in Paradise," season 6, episode 12) in which Kim Kardashian loses an earring with an approximate value of $75,000 while vacationing in Bora Bora. "There are people dying, Kim" is the retort her sister Kourtney gives when Kim cries hysterically.

"But maybe boredom is erotic, when women do it, for men" is from Margaret Atwood's novel *The Handmaid's Tale* (1985).

In "I Intend to Outlast," the phrase "everything Black, I root for" is a bastardization of comments made by writer/actress Issa Rae on the 2017 Emmy Awards red carpet. The poem ends with a line from Morgan Parker's poem "Who Speaks for the Earth?" from her collection *Magical Negro* (Tin House, 2019).

The title of "There's a lot of baggage that comes with us, but it's like Luis Vuitton baggage (you always want it)" is spoken by Kim Kardashian in the series premiere episode of *Keeping Up with the Kardashians*, "I'm Watching You" (season 1, episode 1).

In "New Black Venus," the line "when I go blonde I'm like / a whole other ethnicity" is inspired by comments made by Kim Kardashian during a red carpet interview with E! News in 2009. About her new hair color she said, "Everyone is loving it. They say I look like a different ethnicity, and nobody's been recognizing me."

"The Kardashians for a Better America" is inspired by the free mobile video game *Kim Kardashian: Hollywood*, available on iOS and Android devices as of 2014.

The title "Now that I've survived, when does living begin?" is a line lifted from Derrick Austin's poem "My Education" in *Tenderness* (BOA Editions, 2021).

In "I'm Not the Queen of the Selfie," the line "she stretches a T / like a crucifix" is a nod to a line in the song "Biking (Solo)" by Frank Ocean.

"Who Will Save Kim Kardashian?" is inspired by the rehashed "feud" between Kim Kardashian, her then-husband Kanye West, and pop star Taylor Swift. Disparaging lyrics against Swift in West's song "Famous" prompted Kardashian to publicly defend her husband and accuse Swift's publicity team of lying to hide the fact that she had given West permission to write the lyrics. The phrase "short wavelengths" is a play on phrasing in lyrics by Fiona Apple in the song "Anything We Want" from her 2012 album *The Idler Wheel...*

In "I Intend to Outlast," the phrase "a little stoned & weepy" is a line from the poem "It's Dissociating Season" by Precious Okoyomon, published by Lambda Literary's Poetry Spotlight series in 2017.

"Black, or The Natural World Doesn't Know Me" owes a great debt to the poem "Iris Song" by Rickey Laurentiis, originally published online in the 2020 Shelter in Poems Initiative by the Academy of American Poets. "Iris Song" opens with the lines "You go outside and the trees don't know / You're black," which sparked the beginnings of "Black, or The Natural World . . ." Lyrics from the song "Weird Fishes/Arpeggi" by the band Radiohead from their album *In Rainbows* (2007) conclude the poem.

"Nothing Is Promised" is after the song of the same name by Mike WiLL Made-It and Rihanna and is also inspired by Tiana Clark's "BBHMM" from her collection *I Can't Talk About the Trees Without the Blood* (University of Pittsburgh Press, 2018).

"I can't dwell?!?" is inspired by the October 2, 2016, incident in which Kim Kardashian, while attending Paris Fashion Week, was robbed at gunpoint of $10 million worth of jewelry by five individuals dressed as police officers when they gained access to the luxury apartment building in which she was staying.

The title "The new american girl doll is no longer a slave" is after a line from Precious Okoyomon's "I finally Understand what Drake is Talking about & It's depressing as Fuck," published in the online edition of *The Believer* (2017).

WISCONSIN POETRY SERIES

Sean Bishop and Jesse Lee Kercheval, series editors
Ronald Wallace, founding series editor

How the End First Showed (B) • D. M. Aderibigbe

New Jersey (B) • Betsy Andrews

Salt (B) • Renée Ashley

Horizon Note (B) • Robin Behn

About Crows (FP) • Craig Blais

Mrs. Dumpty (FP) • Chana Bloch

Shopping, or The End of Time (FP) •
Emily Bludworth de Barrios

The Declarable Future (4L) • Jennifer Boyden

The Mouths of Grazing Things (B) •
Jennifer Boyden

Help Is on the Way (4L) • John Brehm

No Day at the Beach • John Brehm

Sea of Faith (B) • John Brehm

Reunion (FP) • Fleda Brown

Brief Landing on the Earth's Surface (B) •
Juanita Brunk

Ejo: Poems, Rwanda, 1991–1994 (FP) •
Derick Burleson

Jagged with Love (B) • Susanna Childress

Almost Nothing to Be Scared Of (4L) •
David Clewell

The Low End of Higher Things • David Clewell

Now We're Getting Somewhere (FP) •
David Clewell

Taken Somehow by Surprise (4L) • David Clewell

Thunderhead • Emily Rose Cole

Borrowed Dress (FP) • Cathy Colman

Dear Terror, Dear Splendor • Melissa Crowe

Places/Everyone (B) • Jim Daniels

Show and Tell • Jim Daniels

Darkroom (B) • Jazzy Danziger

And Her Soul Out of Nothing (B) •
Olena Kalytiak Davis

My Favorite Tyrants (B) • Joanne Diaz

Talking to Strangers (B) • Patricia Dobler

Alien Miss • Carlina Duan

The Golden Coin (4L) • Alan Feldman

Immortality (4L) • Alan Feldman

A Sail to Great Island (FP) • Alan Feldman

The Word We Used for It (B) • Max Garland

A Field Guide to the Heavens (B) •
Frank X. Gaspar

The Royal Baker's Daughter (FP) •
Barbara Goldberg

Fractures (FP) • Carlos Andrés Gómez

Gloss • Rebecca Hazelton

Funny (FP) • Jennifer Michael Hecht

Queen in Blue • Ambalila Hemsell

(B) = Winner of the Brittingham Prize in Poetry

(FP) = Winner of the Felix Pollak Prize in Poetry

(4L) = Winner of the Four Lakes Prize in Poetry

The Legend of Light (FP) • Bob Hicok

Sweet Ruin (B) • Tony Hoagland

Partially Excited States (FP) • Charles Hood

Ripe (FP) • Roy Jacobstein

Last Seen (FP) • Jacqueline Jones LaMon

Perigee (B) • Diane Kerr

American Parables (B) • Daniel Khalastchi

Saving the Young Men of Vienna (B) •
    David Kirby

Conditions of the Wounded • Anna Leigh Knowles

Ganbatte (FP) • Sarah Kortemeier

Falling Brick Kills Local Man (FP) •
    Mark Kraushaar

The Lightning That Strikes the Neighbors' House
    (FP) • Nick Lantz

You, Beast (B) • Nick Lantz

The Explosive Expert's Wife • Shara Lessley

The Unbeliever (B) • Lisa Lewis

Slow Joy (B) • Stephanie Marlis

Acts of Contortion (B) • Anna George Meek

Blood Aria • Christopher Nelson

Come Clean (FP) • Joshua Nguyen

Bardo (B) • Suzanne Paola

Meditations on Rising and Falling (B) •
    Philip Pardi

Old and New Testaments (B) • Lynn Powell

Season of the Second Thought (FP) • Lynn Powell

A Path between Houses (B) • Greg Rappleye

The Book of Hulga (FP) • Rita Mae Reese

Why Can't It Be Tenderness (FP) •
    Michelle Brittan Rosado

As If a Song Could Save You (4L) • Betsy Sholl

Don't Explain (FP) • Betsy Sholl

House of Sparrows: New and Selected Poems (4L)
    • Betsy Sholl

Late Psalm • Betsy Sholl

Otherwise Unseeable (4L) • Betsy Sholl

Blood Work (FP) • Matthew Siegel

Fruit (4L) • Bruce Snider

The Year We Studied Women (FP) • Bruce Snider

Bird Skin Coat (B) • Angela Sorby

The Sleeve Waves (FP) • Angela Sorby

If the House (B) • Molly Spencer

Wait (B) • Alison Stine

Hive (B) • Christina Stoddard

The Red Virgin: A Poem of Simone Weil (B) •
    Stephanie Strickland

The Room Where I Was Born (B) • Brian Teare

Fragments in Us: Recent and Earlier Poems (FP) •
    Dennis Trudell

Girl's Guide to Leaving • Laura Villareal

The Apollonia Poems (4L) • Judith Vollmer

Level Green (B) • Judith Vollmer

Reactor • Judith Vollmer

The Sound Boat: New and Selected Poems (4L) •
    Judith Vollmer

Voodoo Inverso (FP) • Mark Wagenaar

Hot Popsicles • Charles Harper Webb

Liver (FP) • Charles Harper Webb

The Blue Hour (B) • Jennifer Whitaker

American Sex Tape (B) • Jameka Williams

Centaur (B) • Greg Wrenn

Pocket Sundial (B) • Lisa Zeidner